my Book Grade 1

Modules 5-6

Authors and Advisors

Alma Flor Ada • Kylene Beers • F. Isabel Campoy
Joyce Armstrong Carroll • Nathan Clemens
Anne Cunningham • Martha C. Hougen • Tyrone C. Howard
Elena Izquierdo • Carol Jago • Erik Palmer
Robert E. Probst • Shane Templeton • Julie Washington

Contributing Consultants

David Dockterman • Jill Eggleton

Printed in the U.S.A.

ISBN   978-0-358-46146-3

4 5 6 7 8 9 10   0877   29 28 27 26 25 24 23 22

4500845355

r1.21

MODULE 5

Now You See It, Now You Don't

MODULE 6

Celebrate America

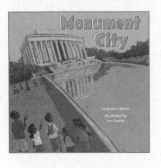

Now You See It, Now You Don't

"Where there is sunshine, there is also shade."

—Kashmiri Proverb

Why do light and dark come and go?

Get Curious Video

Words About Light and Dark

Complete the Vocabulary Network to show what you know about the words.

solar
Meaning: If something is **solar**, it has to do with the sun.

Synonyms and Antonyms	Drawing

period

Meaning: A **period** is an amount of time.

Synonyms and Antonyms	Drawing

orbit

Meaning: When things **orbit**, they move around something in a circle.

Synonyms and Antonyms	Drawing

Super Shadows!

What is a shadow?

The sun shines and makes light.
Light goes through clear things,
like windows.
Light can't go through things
that are opaque.
You can't see through opaque
things, like you!
When something blocks light,
it makes a dark shape.

That's a shadow!

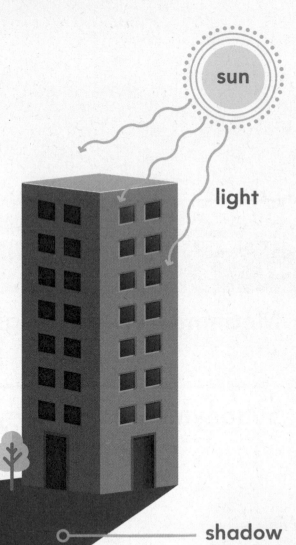

sun

light

shadow

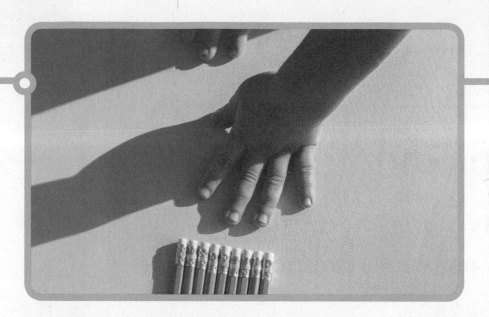

Fun Fact

Your shadow can be in front.
Sometimes it is behind you!

Prepare to Read

GENRE STUDY **Fantasy** stories have made-up events that could not really happen. Look for:

• animal characters that talk or act like people

• a problem and resolution

• ways the pictures help you understand

SET A PURPOSE Read to make smart guesses, or **inferences**, about things the author does not say. Use what you already know and clues in the text and pictures to help you.

POWER WORDS

bank

trembling

relief

nibbled

scrambled

tight

Meet Philippa Leathers.

8

THE BLACK RABBIT

by Philippa Leathers

RABBIT WOKE UP ONE MORNING and stepped out of
his burrow into the bright sunlight. It was a beautiful day.

But something was wrong. He was not alone.

Rabbit was scared. "Go away, Black Rabbit!" he cried.

But the Black Rabbit did not move.

Rabbit ran.
But the Black Rabbit
was right behind him.

Rabbit ran even faster.

The Black Rabbit won't find me here! thought Rabbit, and he hid behind a tree.

But when Rabbit stepped out from behind the tree…

13

there was the Black Rabbit right in front of him!

14

Maybe he is not a good swimmer like me, thought Rabbit, and he jumped into the river and swam to the other side.

But as he pulled himself up onto the bank…

15

the Black Rabbit climbed out of the water, too!

"What do you want?" cried Rabbit, trembling.
"Why are you following me?"

But the Black Rabbit did not reply.

17

Rabbit began to run again, faster than he had ever run before—straight into the deep, dark wood.

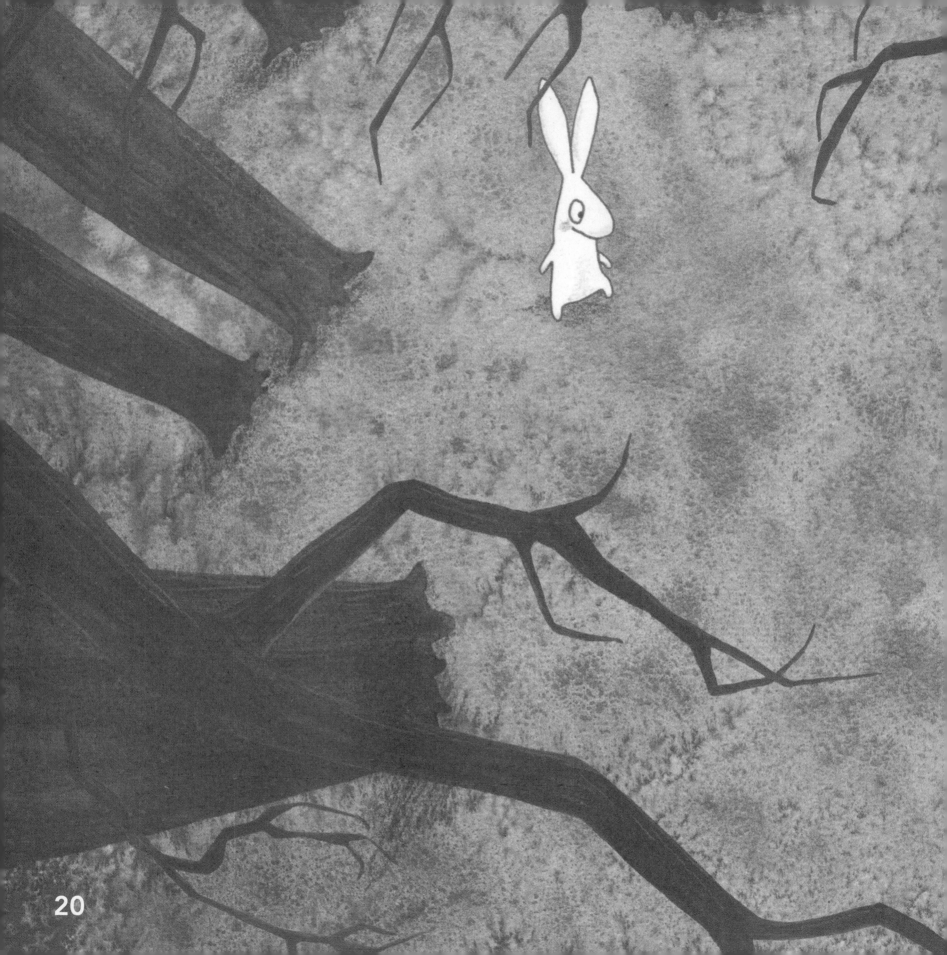

The forest was dark and quiet.
The Black Rabbit was nowhere to be seen.

With a sigh of relief,
Rabbit sat down and
nibbled a carrot…

until he noticed two eyes shining brightly in the dark.
OH, NO, thought Rabbit. *The Black Rabbit has found me.*

But it was NOT the Black Rabbit.

24

Rabbit ran as fast as he could out of the deep, dark forest, with Wolf close behind him.

Then he tripped!

Rabbit scrambled to his feet, but it was too late.
He shut his eyes tight and waited for Wolf to attack…

But nothing happened.

Because there, standing in the sunlight behind Rabbit, was the Black Rabbit.

29

Rabbit smiled, and somehow he knew
that the Black Rabbit was smiling back.

Hand in hand, they bounced off across
the field.

30

THE
BLACK
RABBIT

Use details from **The Black Rabbit** to answer these questions with a partner.

1. **Make Inferences** Does Rabbit know what the Black Rabbit is? How can you tell?

2. Describe how and why Rabbit's feelings about the Black Rabbit change.

Talking Tip

Complete the sentence to add your own idea to what others say.

My idea is _____.

Write a Description

PROMPT Why doesn't the Black Rabbit go into the forest with Rabbit? Use details from the words and pictures to describe what really happens.

PLAN First, write words that describe what it is like in the forest.

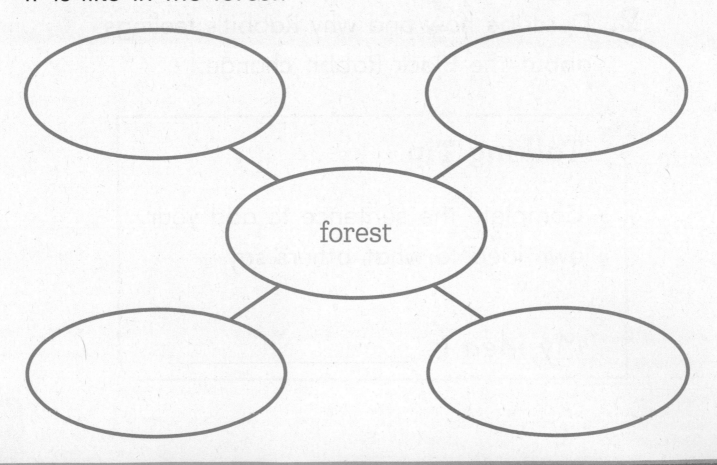

forest

WRITE Now write sentences to describe why the Black Rabbit does not go into the forest. Remember to:

- Add details about light and dark.

- Use describing words.

_____

_____

_____

_____

_____

_____

_____

_____

_____

_____

Prepare to Read

GENRE STUDY **Informational text** is nonfiction. It gives facts about a topic. Look for:

- headings that stand out
- diagrams with labels
- photographs

POWER WORDS
faces
shines
fades
pattern

SET A PURPOSE Make a good guess, or **prediction**, about what the text will be about. Use the text features, like headings, to help you predict. Read to see if you are right. If not, make a new prediction.

**Build Background:
Patterns in Nature**

Day and Night

by Margaret Hall

Day or Night?

Look outside.

The sun lights the sky.

It is day.

But night is coming soon.

What makes day and night?

Earth spins, or rotates.
A full spin takes 24 hours,
or one whole day.
Day changes to night and
night to day as Earth spins.

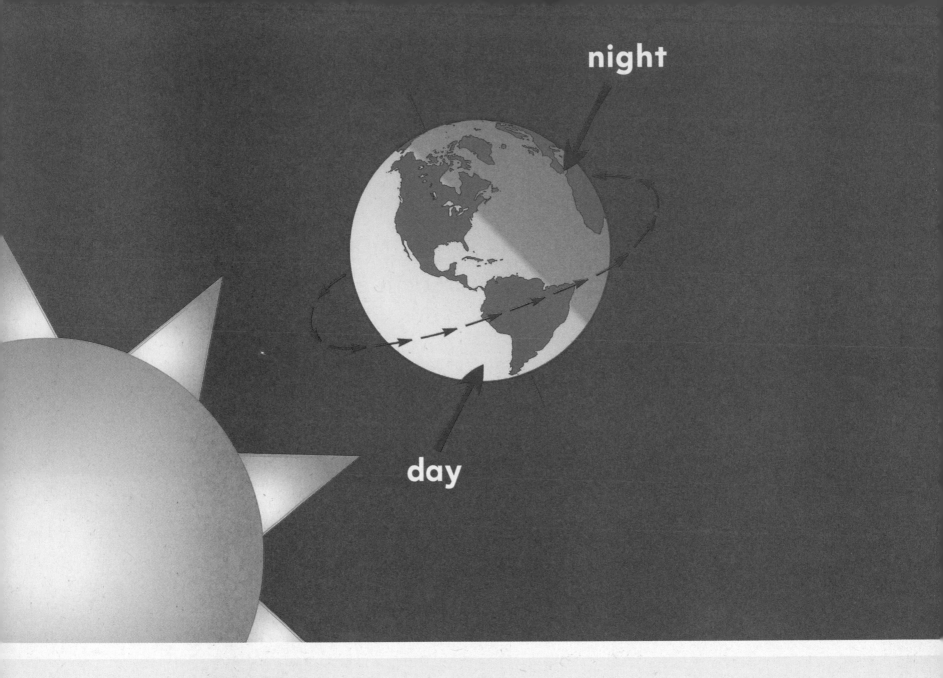

Part of Earth faces the sun.

That part has day.

The other side faces away from the sun.

It is night there.

It's Day

The sun shines highest in the sky at noon.
Sunshine warms Earth during the day.
Sunlight helps plants grow.

Earth keeps spinning.
The part of Earth that had
day turns away from the sun.
The light fades in the sky
as the sun sets.

It's Night

Now the sky is dark.

The moon and stars glow.

People turn on lights to help them see.

Night is longest in the winter.

Nocturnal animals hunt at night.
Owls can see mice in the dark.
Other animals sleep at night.

You sleep at night too.
Most people do.
When day comes again,
it's time to wake up.

It's a Pattern

Each day, the sun rises and sets.
Night turning to day is a pattern.
It happens again and again.

sunrise

day

sunset

night

READ
Together

Day and
Night
by Margaret Hall

Use details from **Day and Night** to answer
these questions with a partner.

1. **Make and Confirm Predictions** How
did using the headings and other text
features help you make predictions before
and as you read? What were you right
about? What was different?

2. How would things be different if we
only had day and no night?

Listening Tip

Listen carefully. Think about what
your partner is saying.

Write an Explanation

PROMPT Why do we have day and night? Use details from the words, photos, and diagram in **Day and Night** to explain.

PLAN First, draw pictures to show why we have day and night.

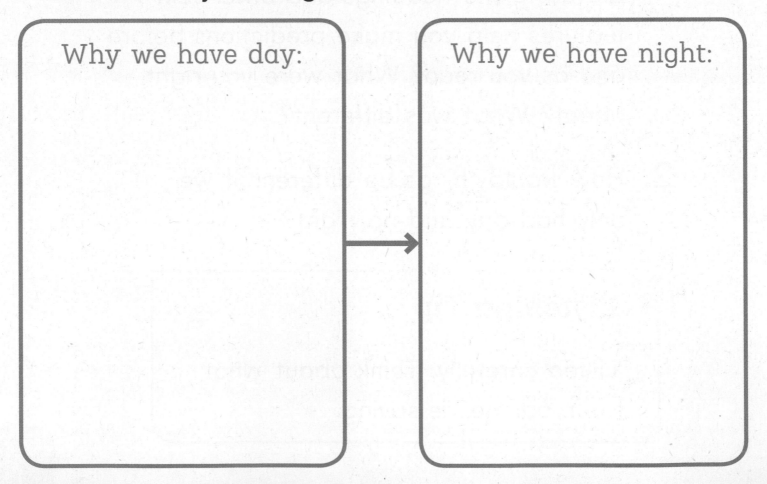

Why we have day:

Why we have night:

WRITE Now write sentences to explain why we have day and night. Remember to:

- Add describing words and details to make your facts clear.

- Tell information in an order that makes sense.

Prepare to Read

GENRE STUDY **Opinion writing** tells an author's thoughts, beliefs, or ideas about a topic. Look for:

- reasons that support an opinion
- the word **because**, which tells you that a reason is being given

SET A PURPOSE **Make connections** as you read. Find ways that ideas in this text are the same as things in your life and other texts you have read. Find ways they are different, too!

Meet Nina Crews.

The Best Season

by Nina Crews

A year has four seasons—winter, spring, summer, and fall. But which season is the best of all?

Winter is the best season. I love it!

I love winter because the weather is cold. Ice sparkles on the trees. The wind makes my nose cold. Cold winter days are great for ice-skating.

Winter is the best season because it snows! The snowflakes look pretty as they fall. Snow covers cars and houses and trees.

It is fun to sled. It is
fun to make snowmen!

53

I like winter because it is a time to rest. Winter days are short. The sun sets early. Winter nights are perfect for hot chocolate and reading books. It is cozy and warm.

Those are good reasons to like winter. What about summer? I think summer is the **best** season. Here are my reasons.

Summer days are sunny. The sun makes flowers grow. Trees get leafy and green. Butterflies and birds fill the sky. Sunny days make me smile.

Summer days are beach days. The sand is hot. The water is cool. We can make sandcastles.

Summer days are outdoor days. There are many good games we can play. We can jump rope and play tag. Warm summer days are perfect for roller-skating.

59

I like summer because the days are long. Summer days slip into summer nights.

At sunset, the sky turns red. Fireflies dance in the air. It is fun to stay outside on summer nights. We can eat ice cream and strawberries. I just love summer days and summer nights!

Every season can be fun.
What is your favorite season?

Winter!

Summer!

62

Turn and Talk

Use details from **The Best Season** to answer these questions with a partner.

1. Make Connections How are **The Best Season** and **Day and Night** the same? How are the two texts different?

2. What is each girl in **The Best Season** trying to get you to agree with?

Listening Tip

You learn from others by listening carefully. Think about what your partner says and what you learn.

Write an Opinion

PROMPT Which person do you agree with in **The Best Season**? Use details from the text to explain why. What are your own reasons for liking that season?

PLAN First, write the season and reasons why you agree with the person you chose.

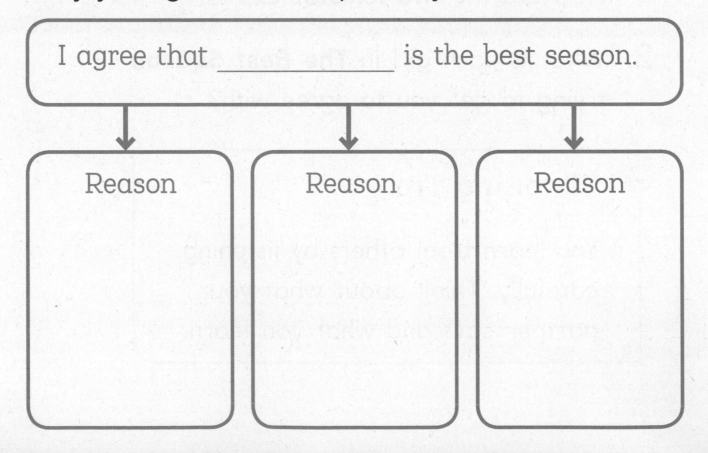

I agree that _____ is the best season.

Reason | Reason | Reason

WRITE Now write sentences telling why you agree with the person. Then add your own reason for liking that season. Remember to:

- Tell your opinion.

- Use **because** when you write your reasons.

_____

_____

_____

_____

_____

_____

_____

_____

_____

_____

Prepare to Read

GENRE STUDY **Fantasy** stories have made-up events that could not really happen. Look for:

- animals that talk or act like people

- the beginning, middle, and end

- ways the pictures help you understand

SET A PURPOSE Make a good guess, or **prediction**, about what the text will be about. Look at the title and pictures to help you. Read to see if you are right. If not, make a new prediction.

Meet Scott Menchin.

What Are You Waiting For?

by Scott Menchin
illustrated by Matt Phelan

What are you doing up so early?

I'm waiting.

What are you waiting for?

Wouldn't you like to know.

Is it big?

What?

The thing you
are waiting for.

It can be.

So it's small?

Sometimes.

Is it friendly?

When it smiles.

Does it have a mustache?

That's funny, but no!

Does it have eyes?

Yep! Sure does.

73

Does it have legs or a tail?

No legs! No tail!

Now I'm confused.
Can't you just tell me what it is?

That wouldn't be any fun.

Is it scary?
I've seen it be scary.

Is it quiet?
Very quiet.

Does it have wings?

It can fly but doesn't have wings.

So it changes?
It's always changing.

Is it old?
It's very old!

I'm so hungry.
Pretty please, tell me what it is.
Is it yummy?

No, it's not yummy.

Have you touched it?

Not me, but others have.

When will it come?

When it always comes.

Is it sloppy?

Smelly?

Silly?

Not sloppy!
Not smelly!
Not silly!

81

I'm tired. I give up.

Don't give up now.
We waited all day.

Will I miss it if I blink?
What if I have to go to the bathroom?

As long as you don't go to sleep,
you won't miss it.

Okay. I'll jump up and down
on one foot so I don't fall asleep.

I'll jump with you.

85

I guess jumping made him tired.

Oh no, I fell asleep.
Did I miss it? Did I miss it?

You woke up just in time.

I don't see anything.

Turn around.

87

WOW! It's everything you said it was.

I'm tired.

Let's go home.

Can we see it again tomorrow?
  Sure, but it might be different tomorrow.

Great! I love surprises.

Turn and Talk

Use details from **What Are You Waiting For?** to answer these questions with a partner.

1. **Make and Confirm Predictions** Tell about predictions you made before and as you read. What were you right about? What was different in the story?

2. How does waiting make the badger feel? Tell how you know.

Listening Tip

Listen carefully. Think of questions to ask your partner to find out more.

Write a Description

PROMPT Pick the rabbit or the badger. Use details from **What Are You Waiting For?** to write clues that describe the character.

PLAN First, write what the character says, does, and looks like.

Says	Does	Looks Like

WRITE Now write your clues in sentences.
End with a question, like **Who am I?**
Remember to:

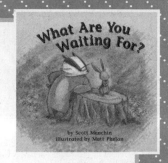

- Describe what the character says, does, and looks like.

- Use a question mark **(?)** to end a question.

Prepare to View

GENRE STUDY ▸ **Songs** are words set to music.
We can sing them out loud. Listen for:

- information about the topic

- the ways words and sounds work together

- musical notes, words, and phrases that
  give the song rhythm

SET A PURPOSE ▸ Listen to the song to find out
the **topic** and **central idea**. Look and listen
for important details that help you
understand the song.

Build Background:
The Solar System

I'M SO HOT

from StoryBots

As You View Watch to find out what the sun is like. Think as you watch. What is the topic of this video? Use details in the song and the pictures to help you understand the topic and the central idea about the topic.

READ
Together

Turn and Talk

I'M SO
HOT
from StoryBots

Use details from **I'm So Hot** to answer these
questions with a partner.

1. **Topic and Central Idea** What is the
   main thing you learned about the topic of
   the video? What are some details in the
   video that explain the topic?

2. How was the information in the song's
   words and pictures the same? How was
   the information different?

Listening Tip

Listen carefully. Think about what
your partner is telling you.

Let's Wrap Up!

(?) Essential Question

Why do light and dark come and go?

Pick one of these activities to show what you have learned about the topic.

1. Be a Poet

You have read about light and dark, day and night, and the seasons. Write a poem that includes information you have learned. Draw a picture to go with it. Share your poem with your class!

2. Day and Night Face-Off

Your opinion counts! Do you like day or night better? Find facts to explain your ideas. Then tell a partner your opinion and explain why.

Word Challenge
Can you use the word solar to help explain your opinion?

My Notes

Celebrate America

"The history of every country begins
in the heart of a man or a woman."

—Willa Cather

What do holidays and symbols tell about our country?

Get Curious Video

Words About Holidays and Symbols

Complete the Vocabulary Network to show what you know about the words.

participate

Meaning: When you **participate**, you take part in doing something.

Synonyms and Antonyms	Drawing

duty

Meaning: A **duty** is something that you should do.

Synonyms and Antonyms	Drawing

appreciate

Meaning: When you **appreciate** something, you are thankful for it.

Synonyms and Antonyms	Drawing

State the Facts!

What do you know about your state? Do some research. Get the facts! Check out these facts.

I live in Texas. It is a big state! Our state flag is red, white, and blue with a big star. The state flower is the bluebonnet.

Texas

I'm from Florida. Our state reptile is the alligator! The sabal palm is the state tree. These trees can grow 80 feet tall!

I live in Virginia. The dogwood is our state tree. It has flowers in the spring and red berries in the fall. The cardinal is our state bird.

Virginia

Florida

Prepare to Read

GENRE STUDY **Dramas** are stories that are read and acted out. Look for:

- settings where the story takes place
- a narrator who says words the characters do not say

SET A PURPOSE Make a good guess, or **prediction**, about what will happen. Use the characteristics of drama, such as characters and settings, to help you. Read to see if you are right. If not, make a new prediction.

POWER WORDS

scene

monuments

sights

grouchy

freedom

symbol

Meet Jerdine Nolen.

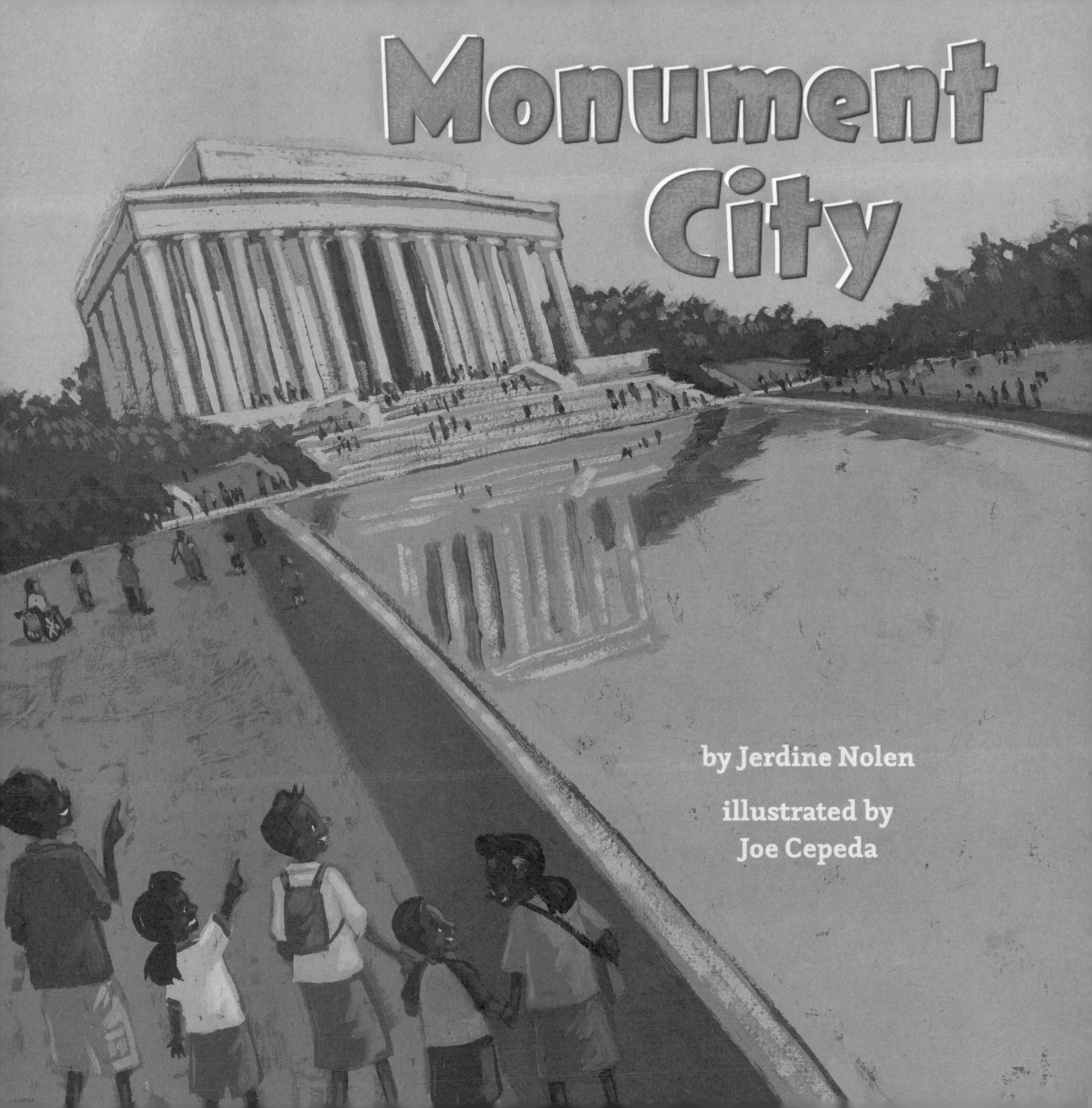

Monument City

by Jerdine Nolen

illustrated by
Joe Cepeda

Scene 1: Good News

NARRATOR: One morning, Mom and Dad had some good news.

MOM: We are going on a family trip to Washington, D.C., next week!

JEFF: Does it have a water park, Mom?

MOM: I don't know. I know it has a big river.

DEB: The Potomac River.

JEFF: Well, what can we do there for fun?

MOM: Washington, D.C., has lots of great monuments. Some are very big!

DEB: We will see all the sights!

DAD: We will stay with Grandma. She lives near the city.

DEB: Perfect! We will be there for the Fourth of July!

JEFF: But I want to go to a water park on the Fourth of July!

Scene 2: The White House

NARRATOR: The family went to Washington, D.C., and met Grandma at the White House.

JEFF: What is so great about a house that is white?

DAD: Just wait and see.

DEB: I see Grandma!

JEFF: Why are so many people here?

GRANDMA: Oh, honey, everyone wants to see the White House. It is the president's house.

JEFF: The president lives here?

DEB: Yes, the First Family lives here.

GRANDMA: The White House has 35 bathrooms and 132 rooms.

DEB: If I lived here, I could have my own bathroom.

JEFF: So could I!

Scene 3: The Capitol

NARRATOR: The family went to see the Capitol.

DAD: What do you think of the Capitol, kids?

JEFF: Oh, no, Dad! Not *another* building.

DEB: Stop being so grouchy, Jeff!

DEB: This is where laws are made.

JEFF: What is that up on the top?

GRANDMA: That is the Statue of Freedom.

DAD: It is a symbol of our country's freedom.

JEFF: What is that tall thing way over there?

MOM: It is named after our first president.

JEFF: George Washington!

DAD: Very good! Tomorrow we will go to the very top.

JEFF: We will? How many steps does it have?

DAD: 897!

Scene 4: The Washington Monument

DEB: The Washington Monument is the tallest monument in the city.

JEFF: It has 897 steps, but we don't walk up. We take an elevator. It takes one minute to get to the top.

GRANDMA: You kids know as much about this city as I do!

GRANDMA: The next monument we will see is over there. It honors our 16th president.

DEB: Abraham Lincoln.

121

Scene 5: The Lincoln Memorial

GRANDMA: If the statue inside could stand up, it would be 28 feet tall.

DEB: Mom, do you have a penny? My teacher said the Lincoln Memorial is on the back of some pennies.

JEFF: Let me see that!

DAD: Kids, walk down to step number 18 with me.

JEFF and **DEB:** One, two, three . . .

DAD: Take a good look when we get to step 18.

DEB: Why do you want us to stand here, Dad?

DAD: Remember this step. I will tell you why when we get to the next monument.

JEFF: *Another* one?

Scene 6: The Martin Luther King, Jr. Memorial

GRANDMA: The monument to honor Dr. Martin Luther King, Jr. is one of our newest monuments.

JEFF: He looks like he could walk right out of that rock!

GRANDMA: Dr. King gave a great speech that we still remember today.

MOM: It was the "I Have a Dream" speech.

JEFF: My teacher read it to us. We made a picture about our dreams.

DEB: In school, we honor Dr. King on his birthday.

DAD: Do you remember which step we were on?

JEFF: 18!

DAD: Yes! That is the step Dr. King was on when he gave his speech.

MOM: Many, many people came to listen to him.

GRANDMA: I was one of those people.

Scene 7: The Fourth of July

NARRATOR: Jeff's cousin and family are going to a water park for Fourth of July. Jeff wants to go with them.

JEFF: I don't know what to do!

MOM: It is up to you, Jeff.

GRANDMA: You can't miss the Fourth of July in Washington, D.C.! It is our country's birthday. We are all invited to the party!

DEB: Will there be marching bands?
GRANDMA: You bet! And when the stars come out, we will listen to music . . .
DEB: . . . and watch the fireworks!
JEFF: Then I want to go!

JEFF: Happy Fourth of July!

Turn and Talk

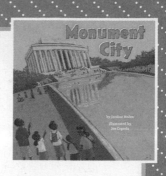

Use details from **Monument City** to answer these questions with a partner.

1. Make and Confirm Predictions Tell about predictions you made using the characteristics of drama, such as settings. What were you right about? What happened differently in the drama?

2. Why is Washington, D.C., an important place?

Talking Tip

Your ideas are important! Speak loudly and clearly to share them.

131

Write a Drama

PROMPT Pick a scene from **Monument City**. Rewrite it your own way as a short drama. Add yourself as a character. Then share your drama with classmates. Tell them what things about your writing make it a drama.

PLAN Draw a picture of your new scene. Include yourself as one of the characters.

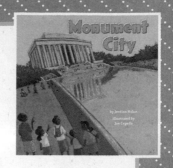

WRITE Now write your short drama. Tell what everyone says and does. Use another sheet of paper if you need it. Remember to:

- Begin with a list of the **characters**.

- Name the place and tell what happens in this **setting**.

- Make the **dialogue** sound like real talking.

Prepare to Read

GENRE STUDY **Opinion writing** tells an author's thoughts, beliefs, or ideas about a topic. Look for:

- ways the author tries to make the reader agree with him or her
- reasons that support an opinion

SET A PURPOSE Think about the author's words as you read. Then decide, or **evaluate**, which details are the most important to help you understand the text.

POWER WORDS

contest

liberty

hope

Meet Libby Martinez.

The Contest

by Libby Martinez

illustrated by Nina de Polonia

Symbols of America

Mount Rushmore

bald eagle

Statue of Liberty

Washington Monument

flag

Lincoln Memorial

America has many symbols.
A symbol stands for something.
A symbol can be a flag. It can
be a statue. It can also be a bird!

Find out about symbols that some students like best. Who gives the best reasons? It is a contest. Vote for your favorite symbol!

Eagle

The eagle is the best American symbol because eagles are brave. They make their nests in very tall trees or on cliffs. They keep their babies safe.

The eagle is also the best because it is strong. Eagles have very strong wings. They can fly 10,000 feet in the air! The eagle is brave and strong, like America.

Washington Monument

George Washington was the first president. There are many monuments to honor him. He is on Mount Rushmore with three other presidents. His face is 60 feet tall!

George Washington

Mount Rushmore

Washington Monument

But I think the Washington Monument is better. It honors just George Washington. It is 555 feet tall. It is the best symbol because it looks like a big number **1**! That stands for our first president!

Pete

Washington Monument

George Washington was the first president. There are many monuments to honor him. He is on Mount Rushmore with three other presidents. His face is 60 feet tall!

But I think the Washington Monument is better. It honors just George Washington. It is 555 feet tall. It is the best symbol because it looks like a big number 1! That stands for our first president!

Statue of Liberty

My favorite symbol is the Statue of Liberty. I like it because liberty means freedom. Many people come to America to be free. They hope for a better life.

America

France

France gave America the statue. That is another reason I like it. I like that countries can give gifts to one another. The Statue of Liberty makes me think of hope and friends.

143

Lincoln Memorial

The Lincoln Memorial is the best symbol. First, it stands for freedom. It was made to honor President Abraham Lincoln. He said all people should be free.

Lin

IN THIS TEMPLE
AS IN THE HEARTS OF THE PEOPLE
FOR WHOM HE SAVED THE UNION
THE MEMORY OF ABRAHAM LINCOLN
IS ENSHRINED FOREVER

Lincoln Memorial

I have a dream!

Dr. Martin Luther King, Jr.

Second, Dr. Martin Luther King, Jr., gave a famous speech there. It was about being fair to all people. The Lincoln Memorial stands for being free and fair.

The Flag

The best symbol is the flag. I like it because it stands for our whole country. The 50 stars stand for the 50 states.

I also like the flag because it tells us about our past. Long ago, there were just 13 states. They were called colonies at first. The 13 stripes stand for the first 13 states.

Now vote! Which symbol
do you like best? Why?

148

Use details from **The Contest** to answer these questions with a partner.

1. **Evaluate** Jade says that eagles are brave. Is this a detail that helps you understand why the eagle is a good symbol? Tell why or why not.

2. Which character gives the best reasons for his or her opinion? Tell why you think so.

Listening Tip

Listen carefully to your partner. Think of what you agree with and do not agree with.

Write an Opinion

PROMPT Which American symbol from **The Contest** do you like best? Why? Use details from the text and your own ideas to explain.

PLAN Write the name of your favorite symbol. Write reasons why you like it.

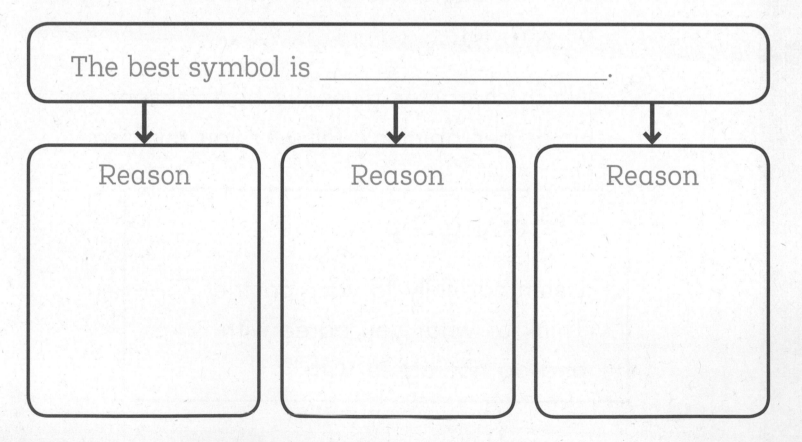

The best symbol is _____.

| Reason | Reason | Reason |

WRITE Now write sentences to tell why you like this American symbol the best. Remember to:

- Tell your opinion.

- Use the word **because** to make your reasons clear.

Prepare to Read

GENRE STUDY **Informational text** is nonfiction. It gives facts about a topic. Look for:

- photographs
- headings that stand out
- the order of events

POWER WORDS

national

towers

base

SET A PURPOSE As you read, **make connections** to things in your life and other texts you have read about the topic. Find ways they are the same and different.

**Build Background:
American Symbols**

THE STATUE OF LIBERTY

by Tyler Monroe

A National Symbol

The Statue of Liberty is a symbol of American freedom.
The statue is of a woman holding a tablet and a torch.

The torch and tablet stand for different things. The torch means she is bringing the light of freedom to the world. The tablet stands for the United States' laws.

155

The statue is on Liberty Island
in New York Harbor. The statue
is made of steel and copper.
The torch towers more than 300 feet
(91 meters) above the ground.

A Gift from France

France gave the Statue of
Liberty to the United States.
It was a gift of friendship.
The statue was designed
by Frédéric Auguste Bartholdi.

Frédéric Auguste Bartholdi

Workers began building
the statue in Paris, France,
in 1875. It was ready to send
to the United States in 1884.

The statue was too big to send in one piece. Workers took it apart and shipped it in 214 crates. The statue and the base it stands on were finished in 1886.

The Symbol Then and Now

For many years, immigrants came to America by ship. The ships passed the Statue of Liberty. The statue welcomed people to the United States.

Over time weather hurt the
Statue of Liberty. By the 1980s
repairs were needed. The statue
was cleaned inside and out.
A new torch was made.

Millions of people visit the
Statue of Liberty each year.
Visitors go inside the statue.
They can climb 354 steps to look
out of the crown on her head.

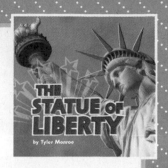

Turn and Talk

Use details from **The Statue of Liberty** to answer these questions with a partner.

1. **Make Connections** Both **The Statue of Liberty** and **The Contest** tell about the Statue of Liberty. How are the two texts the same? How are they different?

2. What part of **The Statue of Liberty** reminds you of your own life? Explain why.

Talking Tip

Wait for your turn to speak. Then explain your ideas and feelings clearly.

I think _____ because _____.

Write an Ad

PROMPT Why should people visit the Statue of Liberty? Write an ad to make people want to go there. Use facts from **The Statue of Liberty** in your reasons.

PLAN First, draw and write notes about your favorite facts that you learned.

Statue of Liberty

WRITE Now write an ad that tells people to visit the Statue of Liberty! Remember to:

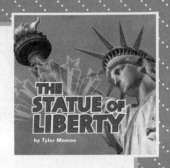

- Tell what the statue stands for.

- Use describing words and give good reasons to make people really want to go there.

_____

- -

_____

- -

_____

- -

_____

- -

_____

- -

_____

- -

_____

- -

_____

Prepare to Read

GENRE STUDY **Realistic fiction** stories are made up but could happen in real life. Look for:

- a problem, main events, and a resolution
- characters who act and talk like real people

SET A PURPOSE Make pictures in your mind as you read. Words that tell how things look, sound, feel, taste, or smell and words about feelings help you **create mental images**.

POWER WORDS

celebrate

share

tradition

parade

Constitution

Meet Pat Cummings.

HOORAY for HOLIDAYS!

by Pat Cummings

illustrated by John Herzog

"Today we will make holiday cards," said Mrs. Rose. "Holidays are special days we celebrate. Make cards for holidays you like."

"I like the Fourth of July," said Hope. "I will draw stars. They stand for the brave people who made America free."

"Add fireworks!" said Ana.

"My card is for Baby Day," said Dave.

"There is no Baby Day!" said Hope.

"Mother's Day is a real holiday. Father's Day is, too," said Ana.

"This holiday is for my hamster, Baby!"

"We will help you pick a better holiday, Dave," said Hope. "I vote for New Year's Day. It is the first day of the year."

"Other holidays honor people," said Mike. "My card shows a great man. He wanted all people to treat one another well."

Dr. Martin Luther King, Jr.

171

Happy Presidents' Day!

"Mine is for Presidents' Day," said Ana. "I like that two presidents share one day."

"I like that school is out that day!" said Dave.

"Can you make a Thanksgiving card, Dave?"
asked Ana. "You could trace a turkey."
"You could draw the first Thanksgiving!"
said Mike.

"You can show a holiday tradition," said Hope.
"Show a big parade!"

"Make a card to honor workers," said Mike. "Draw people doing different jobs."

Chinese New Year

"Make a Constitution Day card," said Hope.
"That day reminds us that we are *all*
Americans."

"Even if we seem different," Ana added
with a grin. "You can make a big flag."

"Make it red, white, and blue," said Mike.

"I picked my holiday!" Dave said. "It celebrates the end of winter."

"Is it May Day?" asked Hope and Ana.

Dave's face lit up with a big smile. He held up his card.

Happy Groundhog Day!

Turn and Talk

Use details from **Hooray for Holidays!** to answer these questions with a partner.

1. **Create Mental Images** Which words help you imagine the holidays the cards show and how the children feel?

2. Did Dave finally pick a good holiday for his card? Give reasons why or why not.

Talking Tip

Add your own idea to what your partner says. Be polite.

I like your idea.
My idea is _____.

Write a Holiday Card

PROMPT Pick one of the holidays from
Hooray for Holidays! Make a holiday card.
Use details from the story for ideas.

PLAN First, draw the front of your card.
Show what your holiday is about.

WRITE Now write the message you want to say in your holiday card. Then share it with classmates. Remember to:

- Write the name of the holiday correctly.
- Include facts about the holiday.

_____

- -

_____

- -

_____

- -

_____

- -

_____

- -

_____

Prepare to Read

GENRE STUDY **Poetry** uses images, sounds, and rhythm to express ideas and feelings. Look for:

- groups of lines called stanzas
- rhyme, or words whose endings sound alike
- rhythm, or pattern of beats from the words
- words that make you think of pictures

SET A PURPOSE As you read, listen for the rhyming words where each line ends. Think about the main topic of each stanza, or group of lines.

Meet Kristine O'Connell George.

Patriotic
Poems

illustrated by Amanda Lima

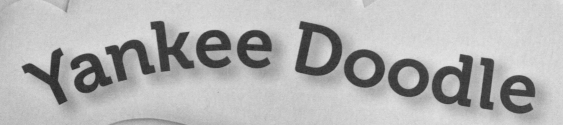

Yankee Doodle

Yankee Doodle came to town,
Riding on a pony;
Stuck a feather in his hat
And called it Macaroni.

Traditional Song

Labor Day

First Monday in September
that's when we remember
to honor workers who toil long.
Their efforts make our country strong.
We give a gift they all like best;
We give them all a day of rest!

Marci Ridlon

A Day for
Martin Luther King, Jr.

We hear the words "let freedom ring!"
And think of Martin Luther King.

A man of honor, standing tall
Dreamed of equality for all.

He saw a world where there could be,
All people living proud and free.

Today we celebrate and sing,
So here and now, let freedom ring!

Kate Arnold

Celebration

Wait here a minute,

I'll bring your gifts—

ribbons for your branches,

buckets of water, and

a wheelbarrow of mulch.

Happy Arbor Day!

Kristine O'Connell George

Turn and Talk

Patriotic
Poems

Use details from **Patriotic Poems** to answer these questions with a partner.

1. **Elements of Poetry** How do each of the poems make you feel? How do the describing words and the rhyme and rhythm help make you feel that way?

2. Which poem has the most stanzas? Which poem has the most lines? Explain.

Listening Tip

Listen carefully. Make connections. How is what your partner says like other things you know?

Let's Wrap Up!

? Essential Question

What do holidays and symbols tell about our country?

Pick one of these activities to show what you have learned about the topic.

1. **A Symbol for You**

Think about the American symbols you have read about. Make a symbol that stands for you! It can show something that is important to you. Explain it to a partner.

188

2. America's Parade

Draw a parade to celebrate America. Which famous Americans will march by? Which monuments will be on floats? Add labels. Tell your class about the parade!

Word Challenge

Can you use the word participate to tell about your parade?

My Notes

Glossary

A

appreciate When you appreciate something, you are thankful for it. After I work hard, I **appreciate** resting.

B

bank A bank is the land right next to a river or stream. We had a picnic on the river's **bank**.

base The base of something is the bottom part of it. The fountain is on a **base** made of stone.

blink When you blink, you open and close your eyes quickly. Turning on the bright lights made us **blink**.

C

celebrate When you celebrate, you do something fun to remember a special event. Let's have a party to **celebrate** your birthday!

Constitution The Constitution is the group of laws that we follow in our country. The **Constitution** tells us what we can and cannot do.

contest A contest is a game or race in which people try to win. She got a prize for winning the **contest**.

D

duty A duty is something that you should do. A doctor's **duty** is to help sick people get well.

E

early If something happens early, it happens before the time you are expecting it. We almost missed the bus because it came **early** today.

F

faces If something faces you, the front part of it is toward you. The house **faces** the sea.

fades When something fades, it slowly loses color and goes away. The light **fades** after the sun goes down.

freedom Freedom is being able to do what you want to do. At the park, we have the **freedom** to run around.

G

grouchy When you are grouchy, you are in a bad mood. I feel **grouchy** when I do not get enough sleep.

H

hope When you hope for something, you wish for it to happen. I **hope** I will go camping soon.

191

L

liberty When you have liberty, you can live your life the way you want. We have the **liberty** to go to any town we choose.

M

monuments Monuments are statues or buildings that help us remember a person or event. The Washington Monument is one of my favorite **monuments**.

N

national If something is national, it belongs to the whole country. Our country has many **national** symbols, like the eagle and the flag.

nibbled If you nibbled on something, you took small bites of it. The mouse **nibbled** on a piece of cheese.

O

orbit When things orbit, they move around something in a circle. Planets **orbit** around the sun.

P

parade A parade is a group of people who march or ride down a street on a special day. We clapped to the music as the **parade** went by.

participate   When you participate, you take part in doing something. All the kids **participate** in the game.

pattern   A pattern is something that happens over and over again. The days of the week follow a **pattern**.

period   A period is an amount of time. It was rainy for a **period** of a few days.

R

relief   You feel relief when you know you can stop worrying about something. The chef felt **relief** when the dinner did not burn.

S

scene   A scene is a part of a play. The first **scene** in the play takes place on a farm.

scrambled   If you scrambled, you moved very quickly to hurry. I woke up late and **scrambled** out of bed.

seasons   Seasons are the four parts of a year—spring, summer, fall, and winter. I like summer better than the other **seasons**.

share   When two people share something, they both have it or use it. It is nice to **share** toys and other things with your friends.

shines When something shines, it gives off a bright light. The flashlight **shines** and lights up the dark room.

sights Sights are interesting places people like to visit. We saw the park and other **sights** in the city.

sloppy Something that is sloppy is messy and not tidy. My room looked **sloppy** before I cleaned it.

solar If something is solar, it has to do with the sun. **Solar** power is made from sunlight.

symbol A symbol is something that is used to mean something else. A heart is a **symbol** of love.

T

tight If something is shut tight, nothing can get in or out. Be sure the window is shut **tight** to keep the rain out.

touched If you touched something, you felt it with your hands or fingers. I **touched** the soft, furry kitten.

towers If one thing towers over something else, it is a lot taller. The tall building **towers** over the smaller buildings.

tradition   A tradition is a special way people have done something for a long time. Is it your family's **tradition** to have a big meal on Thanksgiving?

trembling   If you are trembling, you are shaking because you are afraid. I was **trembling** until I learned the strange noise outside was just a bird.

W

waiting   If you are waiting, you are staying ready for something you think will happen. We are **waiting** for the rain to stop so we can have a picnic.

weather   The weather is what the air outside is like. The **weather** was too cold and rainy to go outside.

Index of Titles and Authors

Acknowledgments

The Black Rabbit by Philippa Leathers. Copyright © 2013 by Philippa Leathers. Reprinted by permission of Candlewick Press.

"Celebration" from *Old Elm Speaks: Tree Poems* by Kristine O'Connell George. Text copyright © 1998 by Kristine O'Connell George. Reprinted by permission of Houghton Mifflin Harcourt and Kristine O'Connell George.

Day and Night by Margaret Hall. Text copyright © 2007 by Capstone Press. Reprinted by permission of Capstone Press Publishers.

"Labor Day" by Marci Ridlon from *Days to Celebrate* by Lee Bennett Hopkins. Published by Greenwillow Books, an imprint of HarperCollins Publishers. Text copyright © 2004 by Marci Ridlon. Reprinted by permission of Marci Ridlon McGill.

The Statue of Liberty by Tyler Monroe. Text copyright © 2014 by Capstone Press, a Capstone imprint. Reprinted by permission of Capstone Press Publishers.

What Are You Waiting For? by Scott Menchin, illustrated by Matt Phelan. Text copyright © 2017 by Scott Menchin. Illustrations copyright © 2017 by Matt Phelan. Reprinted by permission of Roaring Brook Press, a division of Holtzbrinck Publishing Holdings Limited Partnership.

Web/Electronic Versions: *What Are You Waiting For?* by Scott Menchin, illustrated by Matt Phelan. Text copyright © 2017 by Scott Menchin. Illustrations copyright © 2017 by Matt Phelan. Reprinted by permission of Roaring Brook Press, a division of Holtzbrinck Publishing Holdings Limited Partnership. CAUTION: Users are warned that this work is protected under copyright laws and downloading is strictly prohibited. The right to reproduce or transfer the work via any medium must be secured with Roaring Brook Press, a division of Holtzbrinck Publishing Holdings Limited Partnership.

Credits